KU-617-041

CLOCKS
&
WATCHES

ANTIQUES ROADSHOW
POCKET GUIDE

CLOCKS
&
WATCHES

SIMON BULL

BBC BOOKS

A MARSHALL EDITION

Published by BBC Books, a division of BBC Enterprises Ltd,
Woodlands, 80 Wood Lane, London W12 0TT

Conceived, edited and designed by
Marshall Editions
170 Piccadilly, London W1V 9DD

Copyright © 1995 Marshall Editions Developments Ltd

All rights reserved. No part of this publication may be
reproduced, stored in a retrieval system, or transmitted in
any other form or by any means, electronic, mechanical,
photocopying, recording or otherwise, without the prior
permission in writing of the publisher.

ISBN 0 563 37131 5

10 9 8 7 6 5 4 3 2 1

EDITORS GWEN RIGBY, HEATHER MAGRILL
ART EDITOR HELEN SPENCER
PICTURE EDITOR ELIZABETH LOVING
ASSISTANT EDITOR SIMON BEECROFT
ART DIRECTOR JOHN BIGG

ILLUSTRATIONS by János Márffy,
Stan North, Coral Mula, Aziz Khan
ALL PHOTOGRAPHS by Clive Corless,
except the following:
CHRISTIE'S IMAGES: 6; 7*t*; 15; 18; 20*t*; 21*t*; 22; 23;
30*l*; 32; 34*l*; 37*r*; 39; 45*r*; 49*bl*; 50*tl*; 54; 55*br*
SOTHEBY'S: 55*l* & *tr.*
t = top, *l* = left, *r* = right, *b* = bottom

Valuation is an imprecise art and prices vary for
many reasons. The valuations given are estimated
auction prices at the time of going to press.
As auctions take place in the public arena, this
is considered to be the fairest value.

Antiques Roadshow is a trademark of the British Broadcasting
Corporation and is used under licence.

Origination by Master Image, Singapore
Type film by Dorchester Typesetting
Printed and bound in Portugal by Printer Portuguesa

CONTENTS

INTRODUCTION

IT IS EXACTLY TWENTY-SIX YEARS SINCE I WALKED into a bric-a-brac shop in Hastings old town and bought my first clock – a French mantel timepiece costing £12. Unfortunately I simply cannot remember why I decided to buy it, since I was not involved in the business and the sum involved was quite substantial when compared with a wage of 35 pence an hour. However, I am certain that I did not get the idea from a book, since nobody would then have bothered to include such a menial clock in a publication.

I still own the clock, not out of sentimentality but simply because it cost far too much at the time, and for the next 10 years would only have been resaleable at a loss. Today I would admit to being rather attached to it, and in the meantime such clocks have become "rare and sought after" to quote a recent article.

It seems that my first purchase, which initially might have been regarded as a mistake, fits perfectly into the scenario of what has happened to the world of antiques and collecting over the last 15 years, and the pattern looks set to continue. A combination of events – increased wealth, inflation, greater awareness of major events in the art and auction world and, indeed, those early programmes on BBC television – have conspired within the period virtually to exhaust the seemingly endless supply of fine antiques.

I use the word "antique" in the sense in which it used to be employed by the organizers of our most prestigious antiques fairs – any object of good quality and in perfect condition that was manufactured before 1830. These objects have not, of course, disappeared; they have, in many instances, just become prohibitively expensive and difficult to find in the market place. The result has been that, in line with the legal definition, the minimum age for an antique is now generally accepted as being 100 years. Today most antiques fairs and specialist auction houses will judge the suitability of an item on its merit, rather than its period.

The purpose of this pocket guide, which notably does not include the word "antique" in the title, is therefore to try to provide a brief historical outline of the types of clocks and watches most frequently seen at the *Antiques Roadshow* recordings, for these are what most people have in their homes. The illustrations are mainly of items that have been brought along to the programme, including those occasional "finds" that turn up every so often, and with a selection of particular rarities from other sources included to illustrate a point.

Having appeared on the Roadshow as a guest for more years than I would care to admit, my lasting impression is of the way in which people's attitudes have changed toward things that are old. Certainly, expert and visitor alike still harbour a flicker of hope that inside every newspaper parcel is a discovery waiting to be made, but in reality people now have more curiosity and interest in knowing the age and origins of their possessions and in the means of conserving them. It would be satisfying to believe that this short guide will be of help in doing this.

7

HISTORICAL SURVEY

The first clocks found in large enough quantities to interest the collector are the mid-16th century table clocks made in Augsburg and Nuremberg.

In 1657–58 the Dutchman Christiaan Huygens devised the pendulum, which revolutionized the timekeeping of clocks. The balance hairspring had a similar effect on watches and portable clocks. So by the end of the 1600s the problem of making fairly accurate domestic clocks and watches had been solved.

London became the centre for the best clocks and watches, and this was the period of the great English clockmakers: East, Fromanteel, Graham, Knibb, Quare and Tompion. English movements exported to Holland were housed in locally made cases, while complete clocks were sent to the rest of Europe, to Turkey and even to China.

As maritime trade grew, so did the need for precision timekeeping. In the late 1700s, the quest was pursued in England and France, culminating in the work of the greatest watchmaker ever, Abraham-Louis Breguet.

In the 1800s, the English stuck to producing handmade clocks, while the French made carriage and mantel clocks with standardized movements. After the middle of the century, both were overtaken by mass-produced clocks from Germany and the U.S. and watches from Switzerland.

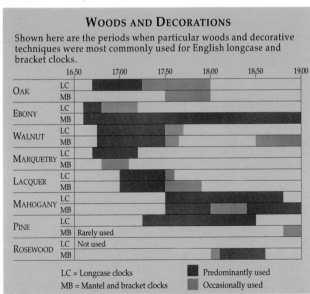

WOODS AND DECORATIONS

Shown here are the periods when particular woods and decorative techniques were most commonly used for English longcase and bracket clocks.

LC = Longcase clocks
MB = Mantel and bracket clocks

Predominantly used
Occasionally used

SHAPES OF CLOCKS

1 BRONZE WALL CLOCK

2 TAVERN CLOCK

3 LONGCASE CLOCK

4 CARRIAGE CLOCK

5 LANTERN CLOCK

6 STATION DIAL CLOCK

7 SKELETON CLOCK

Clocks came in a variety of shapes to suit their intended location and their function. **1** Grand bronze wall clock that may have decorated an 18th-C French interior; also popular in the 19th C. **2** 18th-C tavern, or Act of Parliament, clock. **3** English longcase clock of imposing 18th-C design.

4 Classic French carriage clock, of the type made from *c.*1850. **5** Lantern clock, the first English household clock, made from *c.*1620. **6** Dial clock of the type found on railway stations from *c.*1850. **7** Elegant and complicated French skeleton clock of the Empire period; early 19th C.

How Clocks Work

By the mid-1500s, small table clocks were being made with the movement held between two plates, cut to the same shape and size as the case, and with the dial on top. In the mid-1600s, this construction was adapted to a vertical format for the movements of bracket and longcase clocks. Since then, most clock movements have been of the plated type.

The same is true of watches, except that, in the 1760s, the Frenchman J.A. Lepine invented a system of thin metal braces for each wheel in the train, which allowed much slimmer watches to be made.

The functions of a clock or watch – striking the hours, for instance – are controlled by various "trains", which are incorporated within the movement. A train is a series of gear wheels and pinions running

The Motive Power of Clocks

The first type of escapement was the **verge escapement**, known also as a crown-wheel escapement because the teeth were cut to look like a crown.

In the **anchor escapement**, developed c.1670, the pallets resemble a ship's anchor. First used for longcase, tavern and lantern clocks with a second-beating long pendulum, c.1800 it was used in bracket clocks with a shorter pendulum. English spring-driven bracket clocks were usually fitted with a fusee attached by a cord or chain to the spring barrel.

These two types of escapement were followed by many others.

VERGE ESCAPEMENT

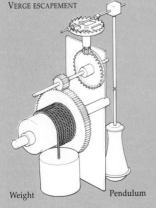

Weight   Pendulum

ANCHOR ESCAPEMENT

Key and Fusee

Spring barrel

from the source of power to the function performed; there is normally one train for each function.

Most clocks were driven by weights or coiled springs before the advent of electricity. As it falls, a weight accelerates, and as it unwinds, a spring weakens; so a device, known as an escapement, was needed to allow only some of the driving power to escape at a time. With each swing of the balance, or pendulum, the hands move on slightly as the escapement is briefly unlocked and locked again.

Some spring-driven movements incorporate a fusee to compensate for the weakening of the spring as it unwinds. The fusee is a concave-sided cone cut with a spiral groove. When fully wound, the spring pulls against the narrow end of the fusee; as it unwinds, it works its way toward the wider end.

The Germans used the fusee in the trains for table clocks; by 1700 the French had dispensed with it, but the English used it until the early 1900s, and it is a hallmark of the high quality of English clocks.

The **brocot escapement**, found in French clocks in the 1800s, was usually visible on the dial. The **lever escapement**, developed in 1759 by Thomas Mudge, is still used in mechanical wrist watches. The **cylinder escapement**, perfected by George Graham, and the **dead-beat escapement**, which he invented in 1715, were used respectively for lower priced pocket watches, and for regulators and astronomical clocks.

CYLINDER ESCAPEMENT

LEVER ESCAPEMENT

BROCOT ESCAPEMENT   DEAD-BEAT ESCAPEMENT

CLOCK FACES

The dials of English and French clocks were markedly different. While the English kept to a basically rectangular shape, French dials were, from c.1715, circular. Enamelling techniques were more advanced in France, and one-piece enamel dials were produced c.1715–20 for watches and c.1725–35 for clocks. Before this, enamel hour plaques in a cast ormolu frame were used – a style that was revived c.1850.

Enamelled dials were rare in England; watches had them only after the 1740s, and clocks after the 1850s. English dials had an applied chapter ring and spandrels fixed to the dial plate; even after the 1760s a flat brass dial, engraved and silvered, was more usual than enamel. By c.1780, "white" dials, painted and decorated with polychrome spandrels and arches, were common on longcase clocks.

CLOCK DIAL TYPES

The design of a dial and the materials used can reveal when and where it was made and for what type of clock. **1** Silvered and gilt brass dial for a single-hand clock, 18th C. **2** Dial with cast scrollwork panel and dark blue numerals on white enamel plaques, 18th C, revived 19th C. **3** German painted dial with brass centre, late 19th C. **4** Victorian enamel dial with 18th-C design.

1 ENGLISH BRASS DIAL

2 FRENCH CAST DIAL

3 PAINTED DIAL

4 ENAMELLED DIAL

THE FACE

A classic early 18th-century longcase clock face illustrates many of the common elements of all clock faces.
1 Second ring uppermost.
2 Chapter ring with numerals in black. **3** Spandrels of cast and chased brass. **4** Long minute hand and ornate hour hand. **5** One of two apertures for winding keys. **6** Maker's signature. **7** Date aperture.

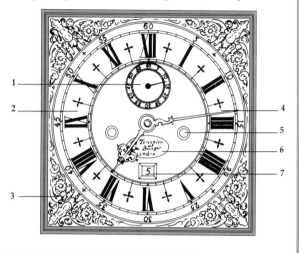

CLOCK HANDS

Early hands were handmade for each clock; in 1690–1740 ornate hands were still carved, but after 1760 hands were often stamped out. Later, the hands were plainer and closer in size.

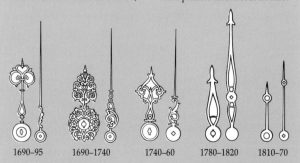

1690–95   1690–1740   1740–60   1780–1820   1810–70

Dials were usually positioned on clock fronts, although on table clocks c.1550–1650 they were mostly on top. Touch-pieces by the hour numerals and sturdy single hands allowed the time to be "felt" with the fingertips at night. Clock dials with a single hand were fairly standard before the invention of the pendulum in the 1650s and, by c.1675, the balance hairspring for watches. Accuracy was thus refined from 30 minutes a day to within three minutes a week.

Minute hands came into general use as a result of these improvements in timekeeping. Second hands, rarely found on bracket or mantel clocks, were adopted on longcase clocks in the 1670s, along with the anchor escapement and second-beating long pendulum. Second hands, however, were not common on pockets watches before 1800.

Calendar hands for the day of the week, date and so on, which had become common on German tabernacle clocks in the 17th century, again became fashionable in the late 1700s and have remained so. Indeed, there was a late flowering in English precision watches at the end of the 1800s, when many pieces were produced with moon phase and calendar indicators and, often, minute or quarter-repeating mechanisms.

SPANDRELS

These ornate corner pieces, used to embellish clock faces and known as spandrels, were made by brass finishers, who cast the pieces in quantity, finished them by hand and fire-gilded them. Spandrels are a useful aid to dating, since patterns were standardized; all the clocks by particlar makers at particular periods bore the same spandrels.

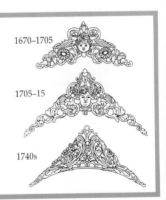

1670–1705

1705–15

1740s

KEYS

Clock keys vary in shape and design, depending on the function they perform and the style of the clock for which they are intended.
1 Typical "crank" key used for winding a longcase clock.
2 and 3 Small double-ended keys, typical of those made for French carriage clocks.
4 Standard brass heart-shaped key for bracket and table clocks used from 1780 to 1900; this design is peculiarly English.
5 and 6 Standard brass keys for English bracket clocks.

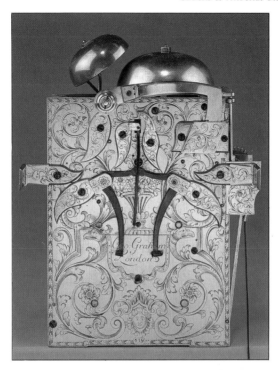

△ **AN ENGRAVED BACKPLATE,** *from clock no. 619 by George Graham, London, c.1725. The engraving on the backplates is a chief glory of English bracket clocks. A plain signature gave way by c.1680 to motifs of scrolling foliage and* tulips, and, from c.1690, grotesque ornament and birds. Baroque scrolls, common from 1710, became lighter and more Rococo by c.1750. By 1800 engraving took the form of repeated motifs on the edge of the plate; by 1840 only a signature remained.

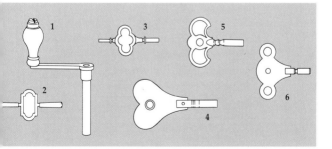

BRACKET &
MANTEL CLOCKS

There is often confusion about the
terms "bracket" and "mantel" clock, but
both are, in effect, table clocks which were
made to sit on top of pieces of furniture,
on shelves or, after the mid-18th century,
on mantelpieces. Contrary to what the
name implies, bracket clocks only rarely
stood on wall brackets. Both these
clocks are among the most collectable of
timepieces, since over the centuries
thousands of them have been made and
wide range of different types exists.
Except for pieces by the top makers,
the price of a good-quality English bracket
clock by a provincial maker can be fairly
reasonable. The same is true of French
mantel clocks, where the variety is
much greater, with cases in the Rococo
period decorated with gilding, marquetry
or ormolu and figures in brass or porcelain;
sometimes entire cases were made from
porcelain in fanciful shapes, such as
elephants or bowers festooned with
flowers and rustic figures.

BRACKET CLOCKS

The introduction of the pendulum into England in 1659 led directly to the development not only of longcase but also of bracket clocks. These wooden-cased clocks derived their name from the wall bracket with which some were provided, but most stood on pieces of furniture and initially were known simply as spring clocks.

Originally most 18th-century examples had a verge escapement; in the 1800s, this was often converted to an anchor escapement, with a heavier, slower pendulum. Movements were framed in vertical plates, and clocks usually ran for eight days.

Similar numbers of cases were made from ebony and ebonized woods as from walnut and, after 1750, mahogany. Very few marquetry cases were made, but some lacquered or japanned bracket clocks were produced in the 18th century.

△ **ARCHITECTURAL–STYLE CLOCK** *made by Samuel Betts a few years after the pendulum's invention. The style, with entablature and pediment, and the dial, with a narrow chapter ring set against an engraved dial plate, are typical of the earliest type of bracket clock. c.1665; 19in high.* **£20,000+**

◁ **GEORGE II CLOCK** *on its original bracket. It is signed for George Graham but was probably made by his pupil, Thomas Mudge, shortly before Graham's death. The "skin" of the bracket slides forward to show a well for storing the winding key. c.1750; 21in high.* **£30,000+**

STYLES OF BRACKET CLOCK

The architectural-style case was superseded *c.*1675 by a plinth-shaped box topped by a dome of changing shape. At first it was cushion moulded (the caddy, or basket top); a concave curved section was added *c.*1720 (the inverted bell top); by 1760 the curves were reversed (the bell top); break-arch cases appeared in the late 1700s, followed by balloon tops; lancet and chamfer tops were in vogue from Regency times.

CADDY, OR BASKET, TOP, 1670–1725

REPOUSSÉ BASKET TOP, 1690–1725

INVERTED BELL TOP, 1720–70

BELL TOP, 1760–1810

BREAK-ARCH TOP, 1750–1830

BALLOON TOP, 1780–1820

LANCET TOP, 1810–60

CHAMFER TOP, 1815–40

In the early 1700s, despite the name, most bracket clocks were carried around the house and so had a handle on top of the case; this was, in the main, retained when clocks became more common. Some, such as the Tompion clock below, anticipating the carriage clocks of the 1800s, even had their own travelling cases.

△ **EBONY AND SILVER CLOCK**
This exquisite small clock with ornate silver mounts, numbered 460, was made by Thomas Tompion and Edward Banger, reputedly for Queen Anne. It survives with its original oak travelling case. It is unique. 1705; 9in high. **£400,000**

▽ **EBONIZED BRACKET CLOCK** *by Samuel Norton, London, with the original, highly decorated case and dial. The movement was replaced c.1880, when gong striking was added. Case 1760; 21in high.* **£1,000**

CHIMING BRACKET CLO

Although it was made in German this chiming bracket clock, in a mahogany case with gilt-metal mounts, reflects 19th-century interest in the classic English tast of 100 years earlier.

The value of clocks made durin this revivalist period is determin by both the quality and richness the case and the sophistication of the strike mechanism. Late 1800s 21in high. **£2,000**

English bracket clocks were made mainly in London and a few other centres; many of those signed for country makers were simply retailed in the provinces.

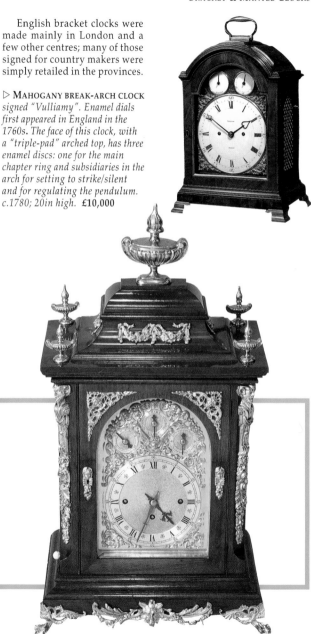

▷ **MAHOGANY BREAK-ARCH CLOCK** signed *"Vulliamy"*. *Enamel dials first appeared in England in the 1760s. The face of this clock, with a "triple-pad" arched top, has three enamel discs: one for the main chapter ring and subsidiaries in the arch for setting to strike/silent and for regulating the pendulum. c.1780; 20in high.* **£10,000**

21

MANTEL CLOCKS

The invention of the spring balance and the pendulum in the 17th century led directly to the evolution of longcase and bracket clocks. Mantel clocks are related to bracket clocks but are generally smaller and shallower and have no carrying handles. They first appeared in France in the 1750s and in Britain a decade later. Before these dates, mantelpieces were not made with shelves capable of taking a clock.

◁ **FRENCH LOUIS XVI** MANTEL CLOCK *signed "Piolaine à Paris", with figures and mounts of gilt brass. Unusually, the case is made of white porcelain; brass or marble was more common. The bezel of the glass covering for the dial is missing. 1780; 14in high.* **£4,000**

▷ **ORMOLU AND BRONZE CLOCK** *by Julien Le Roy of Paris, who was Louis XV's clockmaker. The solid, uncluttered design of the case is typical of the transitional period between Louis XV and Louis XVI. 1775; 11in high.* **£4,000**

ORMOLU CLOCK STYLES

The word "ormolu" comes from the French and describes the gilt finish on bronze or brass. French clocks, furniture mounts and many 18th- and 19th-century objets d'art are described as "ormolu-mounted". The process, which used highly toxic mercury, was superseded by electroplating.

EGYPTIAN STYLE, LATE 18TH CENTURY

ROCOCO STYLE MID-18TH CENTURY

Shapes and forms of decoration were at their most varied during the 18th century in France. Talented craftsmen and designers were attracted to the courts of both Louis XIV and Louis XV, when highly ornate Rococo clocks were made in combinations of porcelain, ormolu, bronze, marble and *vernis martin* – a form of lacquer.

The best makers continued to serve under Louis XVI as well as during the Revolutionary and Empire period, when design followed the Neo-classical style.

▷ **RARE FRENCH PORTICO CLOCK** *with gridiron pendulum. The base and columns are of ribbed blue glass with ormolu mounts, a style referred to as "Palais Royal" after the area of Paris where these clocks were sold. 1840; 24in high.* **£5,000+**

FAMOUS CLOCKMAKERS

The makers' names (below, with dates of working) appear most often on standard Paris-made movements.

H. MARC (1820–60); LE ROY ET FILS (1830–90); A. BROCOT (1840–65); V.A.P. (1840 onward); VINCENTI ET CIE (1850–70); C.A. RICHARD ET CIE (1850–1900); JAPY FRÈRES (1850 onward); MARTI ET CIE (1860–1900); DUVERDREY ET BLONQUEL (1870 onward); S. MARTI (1900 onward).

LOUIS XV ORMOLU AND MARBLE, 18TH CENTURY

LOUIS XV STYLE, 19TH CENTURY

EMPIRE STYLE, 19TH CENTURY

The 19th century saw an even greater production of mantel clocks, since the Industrial Revolution led to the rise of a large and prosperous middle class and an increased demand for luxury items. This was coupled with technical advances in the skills needed to produce such clocks. The styles of the 18th century were revived, but were modified to reduce production costs and suit the smaller rooms of the average home. Victorian copies are, therefore, generally smaller than the originals of the previous century, and sometimes lack the artistic flair and clarity of design.

Most French mantel clocks found in Britain today are unlikely to be genuine 18th-century pieces, since Victorian copies abound. However, 19th-century movements are much more reliable than those of the previous century.

▽ **ORMOLU AND MARBLE STRIKING CLOCK** *in Louis XIV style, with an enamel face. The quality of the mountings compares favourably with 18th-century pieces. Mid-19th century; 12in high.* **£1,000**

▽ **GILT BRASS MANTEL CLOCK** *The style of the case is a Victorian hybrid incorporating elements from the reigns of both Louis XV and XVI. The elaborate scrolls, flowers and asymmetrical curves are features of Rococo decoration. The dial, known as a cartouche dial, was popular in France from 1685 to 1750 and was revived in the 19th century. 1875; 15in high.* **£600–£800**

◁ **FRENCH ORMOLU MANTEL CLOCK** *housing a two-train movement made by Japy Frères and with the original glass dome intact. Japy Frères produced a great many movements, which were installed in various grades of cases. The cherubs on the case of this example are of excellent quality. 1875; 20in high.*
£800–£1,000

VICTORIAN BRONZE CLOCKS

During the 19th century casting techniques were developed that enabled the production in great numbers of high-quality bronzes. As a result, some of the most impressive Victorian clock cases are composed of sculpted bronze figures, animals or objects, with the clock movement an integral part of the design. Favourite subjects included figures from popular literary works and from the mythology of ancient Greece and Rome.

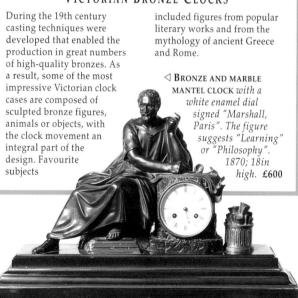

◁ **BRONZE AND MARBLE MANTEL CLOCK** *with a white enamel dial signed "Marshall, Paris". The figure suggests "Learning" or "Philosophy". 1870; 18in high.* **£600**

In comparison with highly ornate French clocks, English mantel clocks usually had wooden cases, with decoration used sparingly. The finest examples, however, were superb quality, usually non-striking, timepieces for the library, study or boudoir.

Wooden mantel clocks found great favour in the late 19th century, when elegant furniture in the style of Sheraton was being revived. The cases, mostly made from mahogany and oak, were fashioned in a diverse range of shapes. Decoration often took the form of boxwood stringing on the edges, or panels of imported marquetry ovals, quadrants, shells and other motifs.

The cases were English made, but many of the movements were imported from Europe.

△ **LARGE MAHOGANY CLOCK,** *probably intended for a large hall. The German movement is of good quality, with a series of sonorous strikes. 1900; 32in high.* **£300**

▽ **MUSICAL MANTEL CLOCK**
A British-made clock, cased in oak, with a musical movement made by the Symphonium company. A selection of different discs was available. 1900; 10in high. **£400**

◁ **OAK MANTEL CLOCK** *by the Glasgow maker James Muirhead, who worked between 1817 and 1841. Indications of quality are the plain carving and the existence of a fusee within the movement. 1840; 9½in high.* **£800**

THE MANTEL SET

By the 1830s the practice
of flanking a mantel clock
with paired ornaments on
a mantelpiece led to the
garniture de cheminée, a
mantel set consisting of a clock
and matching sidepieces, often
candelabra, which enjoyed a
vogue in the 19th century.

▽△ **FRENCH MANTEL SET** *of
veined marble and gilt brass
with a symbolic eagle on the
clock (top). The movement
(below) has a "feather" spring,
invented by A. Brocot c.1830.
1880; Clock 21in high.* **£2,000**

▽ *The pendulum is in a
"spagnolette" (or sunburst)
shape, one of the most popular
18th-century French designs.*

LONGCASE CLOCKS

For many people longcase clocks,
or grandfather clocks as they are rather
affectionately known, conjure up romantic
images of the past. They remain some of
the most popular, and expensive, timepieces
ever made. As pieces of furniture with a
timekeeping function, their cases were often
made by skilled cabinet makers and tended
to follow the decorative style of the day.
The most valuable, and often the rarest,
longcase clocks are those that were made
in London between 1660 and 1720 – the
best period for English clocks.
It was the era of clockmakers such as
Thomas Tompion, Daniel Quare, Joseph
Knibb and George Graham, whose
best clocks, both longcase and bracket,
fetch hundreds of thousands of pounds
at auction. There are, however, many highly
respected London-based and provincial
clockmakers whose pieces are more
reasonably priced. Longcase clocks
always cost a significant amount of money,
but can be an excellent investment.

LONGCASE CLOCKS

The introduction of the long pendulum in the Netherlands in the late 1650s soon led to the development of longcase clocks. These attractive floor-standing pieces, designed with long trunks to protect the weights and pendulum, were first produced in England – where they became known as grandfather clocks. Although they were most popular in England and in America, where they are called tallcase clocks, longcase clocks were produced in small numbers all over Europe.

Early longcase clocks used verge escapements and fairly short pendulums. It was only with the development of the more accurate anchor escapement in the 1670s that longer pendulums were made to beat the seconds.

Since only the wealthy could afford early examples, they were made with expensive woods such as ebony or mahogany, or finished with ornate decoration such as walnut marquetry.

△ BURR WALNUT LONGCASE CLOCK
The date of this clock is indicated by both the arched dial (post c.1720) and the flat-topped trunk door (pre c.1730). It was made by William Webster, a pupil of Thomas Tompion, and has an ogee moulded top with ball-and-spire finials. The arched dial includes a subsidiary strike/silent ring; the hands are pierced blue steel. 8ft 4in high. **£5,000–£7,000**

Although the decoration and finish vary, all longcase clocks share certain components.

Hood

Pediment

Seat board

Fret for sound to escape

Lock

Trunk

Lenticle to view the pendulum

Trunk door

Base

Foot

◁▽△ **PARQUETRY-INLAID CLOCK**
*Both the engraving around the date
aperture and the spandrels on the
face of this walnut clock, signed by
Sam Barrow of London, are typical
of clocks made at this time. Although
the parquetry (geometric) inlay
dates from the 1800s, good-quality
work like this does not affect the
value. However, the unsympathetic
replacement of the base plinth does.
1700; 6ft 8in high.* **£5,000**

The period 1670 to 1720 was the heyday of the English longcase clock. It was also the time of some of the greatest ever clockmakers, including Daniel Quare, Thomas Tompion, Joseph Knibb and George Graham.

In the early 1700s, longcase clocks became increasingly tall. Before about 1710 it was usual to push up the top of the clock to gain access to the winding holes, but after this date it became necessary to make a door in the hood. This extra height meant that dials, which include the chapter ring and spandrels, also grew – a good method of dating clocks.

Most London-made longcase clocks have an eight-day movement, although some were made to run for a month, three months or even longer after winding.

▷ **QUEEN ANNE LONGCASE CLOCK**
Japanned in ivory, the rarest and most desirable colour, this clock was made by Daniel Quare (1647–1724), one of England's finest clockmakers. Introduced in the early 1700s, japanning is a type of imitation lacquer which became a fashionable finish for longcase clocks between 1720 and 1790. Unfortunately, the hood of this piece lacks its finials. c.1710; 8ft 1in high. **£220,000**

DATING DIALS

The simplest method of dating an English longcase clock is by examining the dial for size and for the presence of certain features. Before 1690 dials measured 10 inches or less. Dials of 11 inches were then used until 1715, when 12 inches became standard.

1660–65
8-INCH DIAL,
SMALL NUMERALS

1665–90
10-INCH DIAL,
DATE APERTURE AD

◁△ **MARQUETRY LONGCASE CLOCK**
The concave mouldings below the hood of this walnut and marquetry clock confirm that it dates from the early 1700s. Convex moulding would indicate the latter part of the 17th century. The trunk door opens to reveal the pendulum and weights. It was made by Eliot of London. c.1715. **£26,500**

1685–95	1695–1720	1720	1720
1-INCH DIAL, ONDS RING ADDED	12-INCH DIAL, LARGER MINUTE RING	12-INCH DIAL, FIRST ARCHED DIAL	12-INCH DIAL, ARCHED MOON DIAL

As the 18th century progressed, the expanding and increasingly prosperous middle classes were able to afford longcase clocks, and their popularity increased. They were articles of prestige not restricted to the nobility.

Many of the pieces made at this time were produced by provincial makers as the manufacture of longcase clocks moved away from the main cities. The cases followed the styles of city-made clocks, although they were sometimes as much as 20 years behind the times.

City-made movements, from centres such as Birmingham, were put inside locally produced cases, usually of oak or pine. This was then painted to simulate an exotic wood, such as mahogany.

△ **CHINOISERIE LONGCASE CLOCK**
On the door of this clock, the Chinese-style japanned decoration is raised to imitate lacquer. That on the plinth and sides is, by contrast, both simpler and applied on a flat surface. The clock lacks its finials. c.1740; 7ft 11in high. **£10,000**

△ **GEORGE III MAHOGANY LONGCASE CLOCK,** *made in London by Conyers Dunlop, with a small dial at the top of the face which can be set to "strike" or "silent". The wood of the door shows extremely fine "flame"-patterned grain. 1770; 7ft high.* **£3,000**

CLOCK CASE STYLES

The designs of clock cases reflect the general trend, in cabinet-making terms, of style, details and finishes in the periods in which the clocks were produced.

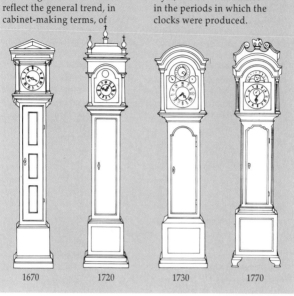

| 1670 | 1720 | 1730 | 1770 |

TYPES OF FINIAL

Finials were of wood or metal, gilded and lacquered, usually in a simple urn or orb design; later an eagle was often used.

The elaborate finials below, on a Dutch clock from 1740, show the Angel Gabriel, Father Time and Atlas supporting the world.

PAINTED DIALS

Although long considered inferior to clocks with brass dials, those with painted dials are now sought after. Painted and lightly fired, these "white" dials were first advertised in the early 1770s. By the 1780s they had become popular and remained so, on provincial longcases, until the 1840s.

△▽▷ **TWO PAINTED DIALS**
The battle scene (above) and figures representing the seasons come from the Scottish clock (right). Its origin is indicated by the spiral columns and cross-banding decoration. Other common themes for painted dials, besides battle scenes, are fruit or flowers, as shown on this West Country example (below).

△ **PAINTED LONGCASE CLOCK**
*Pine cases, with painted decoration,
are common on north European
longcase clocks as is the arched
hood. The mouldings on this mid-
18th century example have been
picked out in gold leaf. 1750s;
8ft high.* **£2,500**

▽ **PROVINCIAL LONGCASE CLOCK**
*The canted corners of the plinth and
verre églomisé (glass with gilded
decoration) below the swan-neck
pediment are typical of Lancashire
longcases made in this period. The
columns on the hood and trunk are
another common feature. It was
made by Joseph Finney of Liverpool.
1780s; 7ft 8in high.* **£4,500–£6,000**

After 1800 few longcase clocks were made in cities; production had almost entirely moved to the provinces where demand was higher. London clockmakers did, however, continue to make regulator-type longcase clocks.

During the Victorian period it became fashionable to decorate the plain cases of longcase clocks with carving. Where this embellishment is of a high standard, like that found on clocks that were carved in the

△ **OAK CLOCK** *signed by George Maynard of Lavenham. When it was made, in the late 1700s, this clock had a plain case, finials and a 30-hour movement. In Victorian times, the case was carved, the finials lost and an 8-day movement installed. 6ft 6in high.* **£900**

△ **CARVED LONGCASE CLOCK** *The Victorians were very keen to "improve" the plain cases of earlier clocks. Sometimes this made a piece more decorative and enhanced its value (left), but the carving on this clock case is too crude. Late 18th century; 8ft 2in high.* **£750**

17th and 18th centuries, this may increase the value of a piece.

By the late 1800s, the fashion for longcase clocks had ended. Other clocks were cheap, easy to use and more in keeping with the smaller homes of the times.

△ **FRENCH EMPIRE LONGCASE CLOCK** *Originally a plain early 1800s clock, its case was later decorated with fine marquetry and ormolu mounts. The dial came from an earlier clock by Lepine, who had been active in the 1700s. 1820–40; 6ft 8in high.* **£4,000–£6,000**

Regulators are precision clocks against which others could be set. Many were made in Vienna, including this example, although they were also produced in London. This piece has a rectilinear case and silvered dial. It also has a rather unusual three-train *grande sonnerie* movement. 1815–30; 6ft 2in high. **£10,000+**

TRAVELLING CLOCKS

The carriage clock dates from the late 18th century. At that time, families would only have had a couple of clocks in the home and these would have been carried around the house to where they were needed. Since the carriage clock was small and light it proved ideal for such use. Although the clocks were not made primarily for use in carriages, when people travelled they generally took a carriage clock along. Initially all such clocks were sold with a travelling case, but over the years most cases have been lost. The variety of carriage clocks is enormous, with values varying according to the complication of the striking mechanism, the decoration of the case, and whether the clock has calendar dials or a complicated escapement. The marine chronometer was another form of clock designed for portable use. It was a highly accurate timepiece which was developed in the 18th century to determine a ship's east–west position, or longitude, at sea.

TRAVELLING CLOCKS

The development of spring-driven mechanisms in the early 16th century enabled the manufacture of small timepieces. At first they took the form of large watches, between three and five inches in diameter, known as "tambour" watches. Accuracy was improved in the 1670s with the invention of the balance hairspring.

Travelling, or carriage, clocks were adapted from rectangular portable clocks, but had the balance and escapement at the top of the movement, rather than on the backplate. They were usually made of brass, with glazed sides and top and a carrying handle.

The first carriage clock was made by Abraham-Louis Breguet for Napoleon I – then on his Egyptian Campaign of 1798 – who insisted that all his generals should have one.

◁ **FRENCH OVAL CARRIAGE CLOCK** *with an enamel dial, made by A. Dumas and complete with its original leather travelling case. It is half-size, which adds to the appeal for a collector, since miniature clocks are generally more valuable than standard-size clocks of an equivalent quality. 1870; 4in high.* **£400**

CARRIAGE CLOCK STYLES

Different sizes and styles were used for carriage clock cases, which had various degrees of elaboration. Cases might be embellished with engraving or set with porcelain or enamelled panels instead of plain side glasses. English carriage clocks are in general superior to French ones.

CORNICHE

GORGE

EMPI

▷ **A STANDARD AND A MINIATURE CARRIAGE CLOCK** *The piece on the left has elegant Breguet hands and the original leather travelling case.*

The miniature clock was made in France but retailed by a jeweller in Darlington, County Durham, although the name is no longer legible.
Standard clock *1885; 6in high.* **£150**
Miniature clock *1890; 3in high.* **£200**

◁ **FRENCH COMBINATION CLOCK** *Unusually, this clock is combined with an aneroid barometer and is complete with its original travelling case. On the top, inset above the barometer, is a magnetic compass. There is also a central thermometer. 1880; 7in high.* **£1,100**

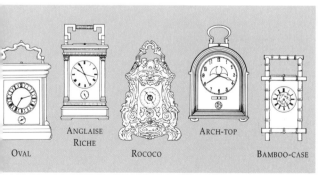

OVAL   ANGLAISE RICHE   ROCOCO   ARCH-TOP   BAMBOO-CASE

The demand for travelling clocks finally took off in the second half of the 19th century, when the coming of the railways revolutionized travel. The greatest numbers were made between 1880 and 1900. After World War I, however, the production of fine-quality carriage clocks went into decline.

The small scale of carriage clocks makes them well suited to the modern home, and good-quality unadulterated pieces can be extremely costly.

△ **ENGLISH CARRIAGE CLOCK** *with a case made of rosewood and a double fusee movement typical of such clocks. The case has been repolished and the dial repainted, which in this case affects the value adversely. Many clocks with an English retailer's name are, in fact, French. Genuine English clocks, however, can usually be distinguished by their use of a fusee and chain. 1850; 9in high.*
£1,000–£1,3000

STRIKING MECHANISMS

The most basic type of clock was non-striking. Others had various striking sequences: hour and half-hour; quarter-hour; and *petite sonnerie* (quarter-striking with a strike/silent lever). Clocks with a *grande sonnerie* mechanism had a three-position lever that could be set to strike the hour and quarter at each quarter; to strike only at the hour; or to silence the strike completely.

△ **GILT BRASS CLOCK** *with a* grande sonnerie *striking mechanism and porcelain panels to the front and sides. Decorative panels were added to carriage clocks from about 1870. 1905; 7in high.* **£3,500**

▷ **FULL-CALENDAR CLOCK** *This French piece has three subsidiary dials (day of week, month and date) and an early original lever platform. It is signed "Dent à Paris". Dent was an English retailer whose clocks were made in Paris. The cast case is ornate for the period. 1860; 6in high.* **£1,200–£1,500**

◁ **LATE FRENCH CARRIAGE CLOCK** *housed in an "Anglaise"-style case, presumably intended for the English market. Multicoloured champlevé enamel is, unusually, combined with Italian micromosaic panels on the side and rear door. 1887; 7in high.* **£4,000–£6,000**

◁ **MINIATURE FRENCH CARRIAGE CLOCK** *with a case made of ivory. The dial and hands are well preserved, but the case is cracked in several places and the replacement brass handle in the shape of a semicircle is not in keeping with the whole. The movement is unsigned. Late 19th century; 2½in high.* **£300–£400**

NOVELTY
CLOCKS

It is impossible to detail all the variations
that have been utilized by clockmakers to
produce novel clocks. Their ingenuity
seems to have known no bounds, and
they delighted in solving complex
problems, only to confound the public with
their skill. Novelty frequently lay in the
form of the case or in automata: as early as
1580 clocks were produced in Germany
in the form of a complete miniature galleon
with moving sailors and firing cannons.
It was from 1800 onward, however,
that the most fanciful creations
proliferated, such as the clock in which a
figure of Cupid on top "sharpens" his
arrow against a rotating grindstone every
hour. But perhaps the most intriguing are
the "mystery" clocks that range from
those in which the movement and
pendulum are so well concealed that it is
difficult for the layman to detect how even
a conventional mechanism works to those,
such as the rolling ball clocks, which appear
to provide their own motive power.

NOVELTY CLOCKS

Made to delight and amuse, novelty clocks have been produced since the 16th century. Novelty may consist in automaton action, an unusual case or the oblique way the time is shown or the clock driven.

Early German clocks were often in the form of animals, calvaries or the Madonna and Child. Many had some form of automaton, such as limbs that moved on the hour or eyes that flicked back and forth in time with the escapement. Picture clocks were also fairly common.

In the 1700s, the French took up the theme of animal clocks and produced fine examples in ormolu and bronze, often with porcelain flowers. Negro clocks, reflecting increased trade with the West Indies and America, were popular in the early 1800s.

By the end of the century, these had been overtaken by "industrial" clocks, resembling pieces of machinery, and skeleton clocks, in which parts of the movement were clearly visible.

◁ **BRONZE MANTEL CLOCK** *This French clock has a silk suspension movement visible through the skeletonized dial. It is set in a lyre-shaped case, flanked by a Classical female figure of very good quality, and stands on a rectangular base with a finely cast panel of putti. c.1820; 23in high.* **£2,000**

▷ **BLACK FOREST PICTURE CLOCK** *A rare, high-quality clock, with an eight-day movement by Sattele Eisenbach. The frame and picture swing away from the dial like a door, and the leopard's eyes move to and fro in time with the swing of the pendulum. c.1860; 12in high.* **£2,000**

◁ **MUSICAL PICTURE CLOCK**
In addition to the clock movement, the frame of this unusual Swiss automaton picture clock contains a musical box, and the lute player moves his head and right hand in time with the music. c.1860; 3ft 1in high. **£2,000**

▷ **WATERFALL CLOCK** *Some of the most entertaining clocks are those in which revolving glass rods simulate water spouting into a basin below. Here, the case is wooden, while the dial and fish's head from which the "water" flows are of gilt brass. 1860; 9in high.* **£700**

◁ **ARCHITECTURAL SKELETON CLOCK** *Clocks with the frame holding the movement reduced to a bare "skeleton" originated in France in the late 1700s, but most of those to be found today were produced in Victorian England; this clock was made in London. 1860; 7½in high.* **£1,500**

Modern reproductions are often seen of an unusual novelty clock: the rolling ball clock developed by William Congreve in 1808. A ball rolls down a zig-zag channel in a tilted tray, which reverses when the ball reaches the end of the groove. This acts as the escapement for a spring-driven movement.

A variation on this type is a clock, first made in America in 1884, featuring a flying escapement which allows a ball on the end of a thread to wind and unwind around two posts set in an otherwise conventional clock.

▷ **LIGHTHOUSE CLOCK**
The revolving head of this French novelty clock, set with a barometer and twin thermometers, is driven by a large spring barrel in the base. Originally the piece was gilded, with silvered highlights such as windows and balustrade. c.1900; 17in high. **£1,200–£1,500**

◁ **THE "FLICK" CLOCK,**
also known as a "ticket" clock, was patented in 1904. It was an early form of digital clock in which cards with the numerals for the hours and minutes are released by the movement of toothed wheels. This example, in a fine brass case, was made in Germany by Junghans. 1905; 5in high. **£250–£300**

MYSTERY CLOCKS

Clocks in which there is no obvious link between the dial and the movement that drives the hands, or with a pendulum that appears to swing freely, are known as mystery clocks. They were popular in France, where numerous clocks with glass dials and cases of only fair quality were made. However, many fine makers, including Cartier in the 1920s and 1930s, produced elegant and elaborate mystery clocks.

△ **SWISS MYSTERY CLOCK** *of rock crystal, gold, jade and citrine, with diamond-set hands and hour markers. It was part of a limited edition recently made by Imhof in homage to Cartier's Art Deco clocks. 6in high.* **£15,000**

▽ **FRENCH MYSTERY CLOCK** *cast in spelter, a cheap substitute for bronze. The face and pendulum swing from side to side in an uncanny way, driven by a tiny pendulum hidden behind the dial. c.1900; 12in high.* **£150**

◁ **"LA MYSTÉRIEUSE" CLOCK** *by the Hamburg American Clock Co. A glass disc behind the dial, with its toothed edge concealed by the frame, is driven by the movement in the base and provides the power to move the hands. 1912; 9in high.* **£150**

WALL
CLOCKS

From the first half of the 18th century,
wall-mounted timepieces were a common
fixture in most public buildings, taverns
and inns. An advantage of these wall clocks
was that the large face could be seen
clearly at a distance. In addition, only the
height of the room limits the height at
which the clock can be mounted and, with
no base or plinth in contact with the floor,
wall clocks cannot be knocked by
passers-by. The earliest wall clocks are
lantern clocks, many of which were
converted into mantel or table clocks in the
Victorian period. These clocks are also
widely forged, so collectors should take
extra care before purchasing. Forgery is not
generally a problem with other types of
wall clocks, however. The most collectable
items today are "Vienna regulators",
the pendulum of which was housed in a
case shaped like a miniature longcase clock.
Also highly prized are well-decorated
examples of French cartel clocks, which
were introduced in the 18th century.

WALL CLOCKS

Weight-driven wall clocks with bulky openwork iron frames in the Gothic style were the first domestic timepieces. From *c*.1650, however, many wall clocks were spring driven.

The first English wall clock was the single-handed brass lantern clock topped by a bell. These were made from *c*.1620 until *c*.1720 in London and into the 1800s elsewhere.

At first, English wall clocks resembled the hood of a long-case clock, and had short pendulums and weights that hung below. With the invention of the anchor escapement *c*.1670, protective cases were added.

Spring-driven clocks, such as the drop dial and the common Victorian wall dial, had the movement box hidden behind a glazed round painted dial.

▷ ACT OF PARLIAMENT CLOCK
This early example has a typically prominent signature, William Scafe, at the base of the dial. The case design follows that of longcase clocks. 1725; 5ft 6in high. **£8,000**

WALL CLOCK SHAPES

The earliest wall clocks had long pendulums like those in longcase clocks and were weight driven (usually going for about 30 hours). The first spring-driven wall clocks with short pendulums (running for eight days) date from *c*.1750.

TAVERN
c.1725–70

TEARDROP
c.1770–90

TRUNK DIAL
c.1760–1830

DROP DIAL
c.1800–80

WALL DIAL
c.1810–1930

▷ **CARTEL CLOCK** *with a movement made in Switzerland and a French-made case, since the French were better at fashioning ormolu. The case style is early Neo-classical, with a hint of the Rococo evident in the angled female heads. c.1770; 24in high.* **£3,000+**

△ **AMERICAN BANJO CLOCK** *with panels of transfer-printed glass. These clocks were first made in the Federal period (1790–1820) in America, and were revived to celebrate the centenary of the 1776 Declaration of Independence. c.1815; 3ft 4in high.* **£5,000**

△ **WALL REGULATOR** *This Vienna clock, with a walnut case adorned with architectural details, was made in the Germanic Biedermeier period (early 1800s). Such clocks have a single driving weight, which frequently runs for a month. 1830; 34in high.* **£4,500**

The Act of Parliament, or tavern, clock originated in Britain in the 1720s. The name derives from an Act of 1797 taxing all clocks, which meant that many people were forced to rely on clocks in inns and taverns. The tax threatened to put clockmakers out of business, however, and was repealed a year later.

In the mid-1700s, a cottage industry in the Black Forest of Germany made clocks with wooden movements and cases that led to the cuckoo clock. By contrast, Viennese clockmakers in the early 1800s produced precision wall regulators with fine glazed cases and enamel dials. From the early 18th century, French clockmakers made great numbers of cartel clocks, often in ornate cases by leading cabinet makers or *bronziers*. Cartel clocks were revived in the 19th century.

△ **"DROP DIAL" WALL CLOCK** *The elaborately inlaid and lacquered decoration incorporates mother-of-pearl inlay. This piece, in good condition, is equally valuable as an item of furniture and as a timepiece. 1860; 24in high.* **£400–£600**

THE LYRE-SHAPED CLOCK

Made from the end of the 18th century, lyre clocks are related in form to American banjo-shaped clocks. They were used both as wall-hanging clocks and, with the addition of an easel back-strut, as boudoir or bedside clocks.

▷ **LYRE-SHAPED CLOCK**
This French wall clock is complete with an enamel face, cast ormolu decoration on a red marble case, and a velour-covered backboard. It has a spring-driven, eight-day mechanism. 1900; 16in high. **£400**

◁ **"DROP DIAL" WALL CLOCK,** so called because of the small trunk below the dial where the pendulum swings. This piece is made of mahogany and has a fusee movement that strikes the hours on a bell. After c.1870, strike on gongs rather than bells became more usual. The original signature of "Thomas of Lincoln" (an English maker) appears on the painted dial. 1870; 16in wide. **£1,250**

▷ **AMERICAN COLONIAL WALL CLOCK** with a mahogany and parcel-gilt case. The painted dial has floral spandrels and is pierced so that the mechanism can be seen. The picture of a colonial public building is typical of this type of good-quality spring-driven clock, which was made for the home market, not for export. c.1870; 24in high. **£400–£600**

◁ **ENGLISH MAHOGANY WALL CLOCK** Unlike most of these classic Victorian clocks, which have fusee pendulum movements, this one has a platform balance escapement. The glass over the dial is held in place by a brass bezel. The face of this good-quality piece is clearly signed "Penney of Cambridge". 1875; 15in wide. **£400**

57

MASS-PRODUCED CLOCKS

The first clocks that can in any way be termed mass produced were those made in the early 1800s by the Japy family. These clockmakers worked in France, close to the border with Switzerland, and were, therefore, influenced by Swiss working methods.

In the early 1800s, they began to use machinery for making clock parts and slowly progressed to producing complete, standard-sized movements, which were supplied to the makers of decorative clock cases. Prior to this, all clocks were made largely by hand, and the English continued to produce high-quality handmade clocks until well into the 19th century. From about the mid-1800s, however, clockmaking in both France and England was increasingly threatened by cheap mass-produced clocks from America and Germany. Usually spring-driven shelf clocks in wooden cases, with eight-day mechanisms, they were made in such numbers, to satisfy a growing middle-class market, that bracket and longcase clocks were virtually eclipsed.

MASS-PRODUCED CLOCKS

It was an American, Eli Terry, who first mass produced complete clocks. In 1807, having received an order for 4,000 clocks to be made within three years, he built a factory to make the necessary parts, using water-driven machine tools. Eight years later he built another factory, where he produced large, weight-driven shelf clocks. These were followed in the 1850s by smaller spring-driven models, such as "steeple pattern" and "gingerbread" clocks, and the industry took off.

The first American shelf clocks were shipped to Britain

◁ **MAHOGANY MANTEL CLOCK**
by the Boston maker W.H. Young. This veneered eight-day clock with an arched top and fine carving below the dial is of a type usually referred to as a mantel regulator, after its distinctive pendulum, which could be adjusted by hand. 1850; 19in high. **£800**

▷ **"STEEPLE" OR "GOTHIC" SHELF CLOCK** *A cheaply made version of a popular design, this clock has a stamped dial, the glass door is undecorated, and the veneers on the case are thin. Thousands of such bottom-of-the-market clocks were made and exported worldwide. 1885; 19in high.* **£50**

◁ **"REPEATER" ALARM CLOCK**
Practical looking and robust, this eight-day clock by Seth Thomas is unusual in that it automatically resets for the same time each day. The original instruction label (below) still exists inside the back door. 1890; 9in high. **£100–£200**

in 1842; by the late 1800s, they were sold by the thousand, at very low prices, all over the world. Distinctive features of these clocks include an overall sturdiness of construction, the case shapes – notably Gothic or arched – glazed and often decorated doors and transfer-printed panels below the dial. Makers' names are usually marked on the dial, and some cases contain trade or instruction labels.

△ **SHELF CLOCK** *by the Ansonia Clock Co., Connecticut, veneered in local spruce wood which has been stained and polished to look like more expensive mahogany. The print on the door below the dial is probably a replacement, since it does not entirely cover the glass. 1885; 12in high.* **£50**

▷ **SHELF CLOCK** *by the New Haven Clock Co. of the type known as a "gingerbread" clock. The name derived from the raised pattern, which was produced by steaming the wood then pressing it into a mould in much the same way that gingerbread was traditionally made. 1900; 22in high.* **£125**

The main rivals to American mass-produced clocks were those made in the Black Forest area of Germany. Clockmaking began there in the 1600s; by the 1720s it had become a regular cottage industry, and the following 100 years are considered the region's most notable period for handmade wooden clocks.

But competition from the U.S. in the 1850s meant that small workshops declined and big factories were set up. Bracket and mantel clocks were not made in any quantity until the 1870s, when it became possible to mass produce springs, but by the 1890s eight million clocks were being turned out a year.

Most surviving Black Forest clocks date from the 1870s to the 1930s. If unsigned, it can be hard to tell them from American ones, but German cases are stained, not veneered, and a brass hook and pin secure the door.

▷ **FAKE MARBLE MANTEL CLOCK**
In the late 1800s, slate and marble clocks were particularly popular in Britain. To satisfy demand at the cheaper end of the market, the Hamburg American Clock Co. produced wooden-case clocks lacquered and painted, as here, to give the effect of marble. 1890; 12in high. **£80**

◁ **FRUITWOOD MANTEL CLOCK**
Although the clock's architectural style is conventional, with finials and carved roof-tile decoration, its mechanism is unusual: the alarm activates a music box (above) containing several cylinders which play different tunes. 1895; 10in high. **£150**

◁ **"FOUR GLASS" CLOCK** *so called because all four sides are glass. The design was popularized in France, but lower-quality copies were soon being made by Black Forest makers. Although the clock appears to be made of brass, it is probably a mixture of brass and spelter; the lion and the base were both cast in spelter, then gilded. 1895; 16in high.* **£150**

▷ **ALARM CLOCK** *of "steeple-pattern" type. The adjustable "grid-iron" pendulum is marked "R=A", for "Retard/Advance"; when a tiny nut below this dial is turned toward the R, the clock runs more slowly and vice versa. 1900; 17in high.* **£50**

◁ **THIRTY-HOUR STRIKING CLOCK** *in an Art Deco-type oak case, with gilt, stamped floral spandrels in 18th-century style in the corners of the face. It is typical of Black Forest clocks exported to Britain, particularly those made by the Hamburg American Clock Co., whose trademark of crossed arrows appears behind the pendulum. 1920; 12in high.* **£50**

WATCHES

Over the last three centuries,
watches have developed from large,
rather inaccurate objects to slim, elegant
pieces with split-second timing.
Early pocket watches, dating from the
17th and 18th centuries, are highly
sought after and can command tens of
thousands of pounds at auction.
The market for women's watches is
developing quickly, especially for cocktail
watches from the 1930s. The passion for
collecting wrist watches is a relatively
recent phenomenon.
It started in the 1980s as a reaction
to the ubiquity and cheapness of quartz
movement watches. The vogue for
stylish and mechanically complicated
pieces, from both before and after World
War II, has led some makers to put their
most popular models back into
production. While the manufacture of the
Rolex Oyster never stopped, that of the
Jaeger Le Coultre Reverso has been
revived. The most desirable wrist
watches are generally those with both
a high degree of mechanical
sophistication and a good maker.

POCKET WATCHES

The development of the steel mainspring in the early 1500s allowed smaller clock mechanisms to be made. This led to the introduction of portable time-pieces and, later, watches.

The first pocket watches, made in the late 1500s, were fairly large. Over the next century, they became smaller and more elaborately decorated, and metal dials gave way to enamel.

Early cases were covered in leather, held in place with pins; later a shagreen cover was common. The decoration of cases has been diverse, including plain, engraved and embossed metal as well as enamel work.

Although invented in the 1760s, the lever escapement was not used until the 1830s. Within 20 years, it had supplanted all other movements.

△ **EARLY ENGLISH WATCH** *This fine watch, with a verge escapement, has a silver case covered in leather and decorated with silver pinwork. The dial includes a calendar ring and blued-steel calendar hand outside the chapter ring. The movement is signed by Riccard. 1660.* **£10,000**

◁ **PAIR-CASED POCKET WATCH** *Many watches of this period have decorative enamel dials. This piece is embellished with a frigate, and the numbers on the dial have been replaced by letters that spell out "Thomas Baldwin" – its owner. 1793; 2¼in across.* **£300**

△ **GOLD HUNTER-CASED WATCH**
*Supposedly developed for use when
hunting, the hunter case has a
cover over the dial to protect both
the dial and the glass. This cover
means that the intricate engraving
on the backplate is concealed from
the casual observer. Hunter-cased
verge watches of this date are quite
rare. 1820; 2in across.* **£450**

▷ **HALF-HUNTER WATCH**
*The window in the case
of this rather unusual
silver verge watch
shows that the case
is a half-hunter.
This aperture
allows the hands,
and the small
chapter ring in the
centre, to be seen at
all times even when
the case is closed. 1820;
2in across.* **£150**

◁ **GOLD POCKET WATCH**
*Made by the American
company Elgin, this
9-carat gold gentleman's
pocket watch is typical
of the imported mass-
produced pieces of the
early 20th century. Gold
watch chains are popular
and this example is worth
almost as much as the
watch itself. 1900–05;
2¼in across.* **£100–£150**

FOB & WRIST WATCHES

In the late 1800s, ladies started to wear watches as a type of brooch, suspended from a chain or strap. Sometimes the fob watch, as these were known, was mounted upside down to allow it to be more easily read.

The first wrist watches, small timepieces concealed in ladies' bracelets, date from the 1860s. They seemed rather effeminate to men, and wrist watches only became popular when their practicality was proven during World War I. Since then, the market for watches has been dominated by Swiss makers, such as Patek Philippe and Rolex.

SWISS ENAMELLED WATCH

Although painting with enamel developed in France, many of the best enamelled watch cases were made in Switzerland for export to the East. The enamelling on this gold watch shows a lady, whose clothes are set with tiny rose diamonds, on the front and flowers on the back. The case is set on both sides with split pearls, which shows that it was made for the Chinese market. 1890; 1¼in wide. **£750**

▷ **LADY'S FOB WATCH** *Made in the early 1900s, this gold watch combines the quality of American mass production (the movement is by the Waltham Watch Co.) with the Swiss tradition of fine decorative cases. The enamelled case is set with diamonds. c.1910; 1in across.* **£250–£300**

△ **EARLY WRIST WATCH**
Many ways of converting old pocket and fob watches were found when, after World War I, wrist watches became acceptable, even fashionable. This silver Swiss fob watch, made in the 1890s and worn by a woman, was later given a leather strap case. Judging by the size, it was probably used by a man after conversion. 1900. **£150**

△ **MINUTE-REPEATING WRIST WATCH**
When a small slide on the side of this 18-carat white gold watch is pushed it strikes the time to the last full minute. Such a complex mechanism is unusual – most repeating watches only mark the hour or quarter hour – and helps to make this watch very valuable. 1930s; Face 1¼in long. **£50,000**

▽ **COCKTAIL WATCH** *This attractive 1930s diamond-set platinum cocktail watch on a 9-carat white gold bracelet is true to the origins of the wrist watch as a piece of ladies' jewellery. 1935; Face ¾in long.* **£350**

CARING FOR YOUR VALUABLES

ANTIQUES MAY BE BOUGHT FOR THEIR beauty, craftsmanship, history, rarity, or even for their curiosity value. It does not matter whether you are buying an item because it gives you pleasure, or because you consider it to be a serious investment. It is important to see that it is well looked after and properly insured. That way, it can be enjoyed today and handed down from generation to generation.

The most important point to bear in mind when taking care of antique clocks is that, in addition to being pieces of furniture, they are working mechanisms and therefore need regular attention to keep them running. It can cost an enormous amount to put them right if they are neglected. The mechanical parts are delicate, and repairs should always be left to an expert. Always seek out a first-class repairer or restorer; even if their services seem rather expensive, it is cost-effective to pay for excellent work by knowledgeable people.

Even if a clock or watch is in perfect working order, it should still be serviced regularly: about once every ten years would be appropriate for sturdy movements such as those found in longcase clocks; once every five years for more delicate ones.

Clocks can be harmed irrevocably through being left in an unfavourable position. They should never be exposed to extremes of heat or light. It is, therefore, not advisable to leave a clock on a mantelpiece above a working fire. When a suitable position has been found, longcase and wall-mounted clocks should be firmly secured by their brackets, with the base plate absolutely horizontal.

Clocks must be handled with care and held upright by the main part of the case only – never by any external parts. If the pendulum is a suspended one, it should be fastened; a clip or screw clamp is often provided for this purpose. If not, the pendulum must be removed. The weights and pendulum of a longcase clock should always be unhooked when the clock is moved, and the movement taken out of the case. Only the correct, undamaged key should be used to open the case.

It is never advisable to run any clock for long periods when the movement is dirty. Longcase clocks, however, are forgiving, and a properly adjusted longcase movement is a sturdy mechanism that will run for years, even if slightly neglected.

If the mechanism is left to run down completely, clocks can be harmed; for this reason, they should always be stopped before any protracted absence.

When moving the hands, touch the minute hand by the base only, never at the tip, to avoid breaking it. Obstructions should never be forced; try to find the cause of the blockage first and if this does not prove to be possible, seek expert help. The hour hand of a striking clock should never be moved anticlockwise beyond the "twelve" numeral. (There is no danger of moving the hour hand of a simple, non-striking time-piece, however.) If a striking clock shows the incorrect time, it is advisable to stop the movement so that the hour hand need be moved on only slightly.

Do not open the back of a watch with a knife. Repairs to both wrist and pocket watches should always be left to specialists.

If a movement is in good condition, or can be cleaned for a reasonable price, a little home "surgery" can often refresh the case. The following general rules should be strictly observed.

CARING FOR CLOCKS AND WATCHES

1 To improve wooden clock cases that have become dull, first try a good wax polish; if this is unsuccessful use a proprietary surface cleaner. To remove stubborn surface grime, the cleaner may be used with 0000 grade wire wool.

2 Wood, marble or stone clock cases that have come apart should be reassembled with water-soluble adhesive. (Never use impact or contact adhesives, which are impossible to remove.)

3 Clean marble clocks by wiping them gently with a cloth that has been dampened with water and a mild solution of washing-up liquid. Remove any grease from the case with some cottonwool soaked in benzine and wipe the surface dry immediately.

4 To improve dulled black marble, apply several thin coats of black shoe polish.

5 Be careful when attempting to clean metal cases. Brass may be cleaned with non-abrasive metal polish, but gilded metals need specialist treatment. Bronze should not be polished, simply dusted occasionally.

6 Never oil a dirty clock. If you intend to clean the movement yourself, make sure that it is completely unwound before dismantling it. Wash the parts out thoroughly using benzine, then clean the pivot holes with sharpened matchsticks. When reassembling the clock, put a drop of light oil, such as sewing-machine oil, on each pivot and on the pallets of the escapement, but do not oil the wheels.

INSURANCE

The question of insurance is a matter of personal choice, and insurance companies vary greatly in the types of cover they provide, and the cost of the premiums. Cover for valuable antiques can be expensive, but trying to find the lowest quotation is not necessarily the wisest course. Specialist brokers, as well as building society insurance services, understand the needs of collectors.

The first thing is to decide on the nature of the cover you require: the kind of "risks". Comprehensive and All In policies cover only certain specified perils, such as theft, fire, explosion, water or storm damage. In the event of theft, evidence will be required before a claim is met, and insurance companies will ask if the police have been notified.

Another type of cover is All Risks, which represents the maximum cover you are likely to obtain. It will also cover you against accidental breakage and disappearance, but not "inherent vice", such as the progressive deterioration of mechanical parts of the movement through use.

Decide exactly what you want to insure and make a detailed list of the items. It is advisable to keep receipts as back-up evidence if you have to make a claim. Insurance companies sometimes ask to see credit card vouchers, photographs or notes of any distinguishing marks. You may even need to consider a policy that covers your possessions away from home, as when they are sent to restorers or if you are selling them at an antiques fair.

VALUING YOUR POSSESSIONS

If you want to get a valuation for items, it is usually a good idea to obtain two quotes: from either reputable dealers or auction houses. (You may have to pay a small percentage of the value.)

Most insurance valuations are based on the full market price, or replacement cost, of an item. That is why it is important to give your insurers as much detail as possible. For example, where the clocks or watches are kept and how they are protected. If you underinsure, insurance companies are likely to scale down their payouts – or may even refuse to pay out at all. It is now fairly standard practice for an insurer not to pay a claim in cash, but to settle the claim once you have bought a replacement. Frequently you are expected to pay an "excess", which can be, for example, the first £25 of the cost of each claim.

Index-linked policies automatically adjust the amount of insurance cover, and your premiums, every year. But it is still worth checking the figures from time to time. It is a good idea to have valuations updated every few years because fantastic appreciation often occurs with certain periods or pieces.

LOOKING AFTER YOUR ANTIQUES

Insurers are very keen that you take "reasonable" care of valuable items. Ensure that shelves are strong enough to support the weight of the timepieces you place on them and don't keep clocks under a water tank or bathroom.

It also makes sense to install smoke detectors, particularly in living areas, and to have fire extinguishers easily to hand.

If something does get broken or damaged, get the written approval of your insurance company before having it restored.

SECURITY

According to research, 1 in 12 households is burgled annually. But by joining a Neighbourhood Watch scheme, not only can the risk be reduced to 1 in 75, but you could also lower the cost of your home contents premium. The local Crime Prevention Officer will be happy to help you set up a scheme if none exists. Usually you need half the people in your area – whether it is a street or block of flats – to agree to join.

Normally your Crime Prevention Officer will also be happy to advise you if the locks and bolts on your house are adequate. Security devices such as five-lever mortise locks on doors and key-operated window locks are fairly inexpensive to fit and highly effective; they may even help to reduce the cost of your premiums.

As a rule, two mortise deadlocks should be fitted to each external door, and window locks to all ground-floor and first-floor windows. Vulnerable windows, such as those in a basement, should be fitted with iron bars. Additional precautions, such as security bolts on doors, are worth considering, especially where a door is not made of timber or is less than 1¾ inches thick.

Another way to deter burglars is to fit an alarm. This can also reduce your premiums, but don't go for the cheapest quote just to save a few pounds. You should choose a recognized organization that offers local maintenance facilities and a full guarantee. The local police or your insurers will probably be able to recommend appropriate companies to you.

If your home does get burgled, you should report the matter at the police station and to your insurers without delay.

National & Provincial Building Society, whose support helped to make this book possible, offers the insurance services the collector requires. Advice is available from its branches, or call the Freefone advice line on 0800 80 80 80.

COLLECTOR'S CHECKLIST

CLOCKS ARE SOME OF THE MOST interesting antiques, and one of the undoubted joys of owning a collection of timepieces is to be able to sit in a room and listen to the sound of several different clocks ticking away.

But most collectors are equally fascinated by the craftsmanship that goes into making a clock. The skills of a cabinet maker are required to make the case; of an horologist for the movement; of an engraver for the decoration and, often, of a gilder for the finishing touches. Watches can display even more amazing feats of engineering and have the advantage of taking up less space.

The fact that many clocks are items of furniture as well as mechanical devices dictates that any alterations that have been made must be thoroughly assessed before purchase. Small wheels that have been renewed do not usually affect the value, whereas a replacement dial is a matter of far greater importance and may severely reduce the worth.

Today, almost any longcase clock is something of a prized possession, and the days when certain types could be bought relatively cheaply are long gone. Anything costing less than £500 is now a true bargain, unless its condition is exceedingly poor, or it was made at a very late date.

High demand has meant that the faking of all clock types is common. Skeleton clocks, in particular, may be assembled from an assortment of clock parts. Fake patination can be achieved more easily on metal than wood,

and is often difficult for the new collector to spot. The only way to gain experience is to handle as many types of clock as possible.

There are three main ways of purchasing a clock or watch: at an auction; through a recognized dealer; or privately, from an individual. The auction houses in London have clock sales about six times a year, and they can be an exciting experience. Provincial sales are far more numerous. Great caution is advised, however, when buying at auction; both the piece and the sale catalogue should be carefully studied beforehand, and, if possible, expert advice should be sought.

Purchasing a good-quality timepiece through a reputable dealer is often a more expensive but much safer option, since any repairs or restoration work will almost certainly have been done to a high standard. Remember that only the best antiques prove to be good, long-term investments. If buying privately, always ask for a written statement detailing the piece's condition and history.

In general, new collectors would do well to seek friendly expert guidance when purchasing a clock or watch until their own level of experience increases. It can be easy, at first, to miss important details when trying to judge the worth of a piece. A second opinion may prove invaluable, since restoration work carried out on a poor-quality purchase, as well as often being costly, may still not enable you to achieve the full value of the same piece in perfect condition.

TIPS FOR BUYERS

1 It is important to establish that the movement and case of a clock belong together. Regard unexplained screw holes in either the case or movement with suspicion.

2 Always check that the dial of a longcase clock fits correctly into the case aperture and that the seat board has not been altered.

3 An original signature is important, particularly if it is the name of a well-known maker. It is, however, easy to change the signature on painted dials.

4 Original painted dials will show a network of tiny cracks, known as "crazing", even if they have been professionally cleaned and restored.

5 Replacement hands will be found on many clocks because of damage to the original hands. If the new hands are in the correct style and of the right quality, they will not detract from the value of the clock.

6 Check the running time of a clock; those that run for only 30 hours are generally less valuable than those that run for a full week or longer.

7 Make sure that watches are in working order since repairs can be prohibitively expensive.

8 Satisfy yourself that the case of a pocket watch labelled as "gold" really is gold. Some American makers produced cases of excellent quality in rolled gold (a type of plating in which thin sheets of gold are fused to a metal, such as copper, at high temperature, then rolled to form a sheet plated with a uniform thickness of gold).

9 Unless the movement is of particular interest to collectors, watches with cases made from 18-carat gold are more valuable than those of 9-carat gold. American manufacturers often used 14-carat gold for watch cases.

10 Waterproof watches may well have been opened for inspection, so if you buy a second-hand one, it is wise to have it resealed by a watchmaker.

COLLECTIONS OF INTEREST

Ashmolean Museum
Beaumont Street
Oxford OX1 2PH
Telephone: 01865 278 000
British Museum
Museum Street
London WC1B 3DG
Telephone: 0171 636 1555
Fitzwilliam Museum
Trumpington Street
Cambridge CB2 1RB
Telephone: 01223 332 900
Science Museum
Exhibition Street
London SW7 5BD
Telephone: 0171 938 8000
Victoria & Albert Museum
Cromwell Road
London SW7 2RL
Telephone: 0171 938 8500
Wallace Collection
Manchester Square
London W1M 6BN
Telephone: 0171 935 0687

Many fine examples of timepieces can also be seen in stately homes open to the public, as well as in provincial collections.

GLOSSARY

Note: SMALL CAPITALS within an entry refer to another entry.

A

ARCHITECTURAL STYLE Term used to describe furniture and clock cases with features such as arches, PEDIMENTS and columns.

ASTRONOMICAL CLOCK Timepiece with a dial that shows the phases of the moon and other astronomical phenomena.

B

BACKPLATE The plate at the back of a clock MOVEMENT; one of two plates holding the mechanism in place.

BALANCE SPRING Spring acting on the BALANCE WHEEL in a watch mechanism to control the oscillations of the balance. It was introduced to England by THOMAS TOMPION.

BALANCE WHEEL The wheel in a clock that controls the action of the ESCAPEMENT, thus regulating the MOVEMENT.

BANJO CLOCK Wall clock in the shape of an upturned banjo, first produced by the clockmakers Willard during the Federal period (1780–1820) in Boston, USA. Reproductions were common in the 19th C.

BAROQUE Heavily ornate style of architecture from late 17th-C Italy which influenced all the decorative arts throughout Europe *c.*1660–1730.

BEZEL A metal rim or setting used to hold the glass on a clock or watch face in place.

BREGUET, ABRAHAM-LOUIS (1747–1823) A Swiss-born clock- and watchmaker who lived in Paris and invented many of the features that are used in every modern watch.

BROCOT, ARCHILLE (1818–78) French clockmaker who, with his father Louis Gabriel, invented the simple adjustable spring suspension for the pendulum.

C

CARTOUCHE DIAL A dial on which the numerals are painted on lozenge-shaped ENAMEL plaques set within a decorative brass plate.

CHAMFER The angle on the edge of a piece of wood, achieved by planing or cutting.

CHAMPLEVÉ ENAMELLING A form of enamelling similar to *cloisonné*, whereby the cast-bronze body is cut away and filled with ENAMEL.

CHAPTER RING Circle on the dial of a clock or watch on which the hours are marked.

CHRONOMETER Portable timepiece of great accuracy, developed in the 18th C for determining longitude at sea. Chronometers are often mounted in protective wooden boxes.

E

EAST, EDWARD (ACTIVE MID-17TH C) Famous London clockmaker; horologist to the court of Charles II.

ELLICOT, JOHN (1706–72) Master clockmaker to George III who invented a form of compensated pendulum and improved the cylinder ESCAPEMENT.

ENAMEL A mixture of powdered glass and pigmented metallic oxides suspended in an oily medium, which can be fused to metal, glass or ceramics. During firing, the oily medium burns off and the other constituents fuse to form a hard decorative surface. White enamel was often used as the base for clock and watch faces.

ENGRAVING Form of decoration in which lines or dots are incised into a hard surface, such as metal or glass, either with a steel or diamond tool or with a spinning abrasive wheel.

ENTABLATURE An architectural term adopted by cabinet and clock-case makers which refers to the components comprising architrave, frieze and cornice that surmount columns.

ESCAPEMENT Regulating mechanism of a clock that allows stored power in a falling weight or wound spring to be released at a regular rate.

F

FINIAL Ornament of carved or turned wood or cast metal mounted on top of a clock case or other piece of furniture.

FOLIOT A horizontal rod with adjustable weights that regulated the verge ESCAPEMENT in the earliest clocks.

FROMANTEEL FAMILY Flemish family of clockmakers based in London in the 17th and early 18th C who made the first English pendulum clocks.

FUSEE Cone-shaped spool in a clock around which gut or chain is wound in order to equalize the tension of the spring as it unwinds.

G

GRAHAM, GEORGE (1673–1751) Clock- and watchmaker who did much to increase the accuracy of longcase clocks with his deadbeat ESCAPEMENT (1715) and mercury pendulum (1726). He also invented the cylinder escapement.

GRIDIRON PENDULUM A type of pendulum with alternating steel and brass rods that remains of constant length despite changes in temperature. It works because brass expands more slowly than steel so differences in the rates of expansion cancel each other out.

H, J

HOOD The top section of a longcase clock which houses the MOVEMENT and the dial.

JAPANNING Technique originating in the early 18th C whereby European craftsmen imitated Oriental lacquerwork with paint and varnish.

K, M

KNIBB, JOSEPH (ACTIVE 1650–1712) Most famous of a family of London clockmakers.

MOVEMENT Mechanism of a clock or watch that causes it to work.

N, O

NEW HAVEN CLOCK CO. Founded in New Haven, Connecticut, in 1853, the firm mass produced clocks from 1856.

OGEE Double curve, convex at the top and becoming concave at the bottom, often found on clock cases, mouldings

and on the feet of Georgian furniture.

ORMOLU Originally the powdered gold used to gild furniture mounts made from bronze and other metals. The term now refers to the actual mounts.

P

PALLET The acting surfaces which alternately engage and release the escape wheel in a clock or watch MOVEMENT.

PEDIMENT Surmounts the cornice in cabinet furniture and longcase clocks. It has taken different forms, such as swan neck and broken arch, according to prevailing fashions.

PETITE SONNERIE Striking mechanism for clocks which sounds ting-tangs on every quarter hour, and a single ring on the hour.

PLATFORM ESCAPEMENT A complete clock ESCAPEMENT mounted on its own separate platform, notably used on carriage clocks.

PUTTI Cupids or cherubs used in decoration.

Q

QUARE, DANIEL (1647–1724) English clock- and barometer maker, much favoured by George I. He was the first to patent a REPEATER mechanism for watches.

R

REGULATOR A pendulum clock designed for highly accurate timekeeping, often used to set or check other timepieces.

REPEATER Clock or watch mechanism which, depending on the level of sophistication, repeats the previous hour, quarter hour and minutes when a cord or button is touched, so enabling the time to be told without the need to see the face. First made in the 1680s.

REPOUSSÉ Term derived from the French for "pushed out", used in metalwork to describe a raised design created by hammering a thin sheet of metal.

ROCOCO Decorative and elaborate architectural style which originated in France in the early 18th C. It emphasized ornamentation and curving lines; motifs especially associated with the Rococo are rocks, shells and floral designs.

S

SCROLLWORK Curving decoration often found on clock cases.

SEAT BOARD Platform supporting the MOVEMENT and face of a longcase clock.

SHELF CLOCK Cheaply manufactured clock developed in America to sit on a narrow shelf or ledge. Most have a plain rectangular frame and glass front.

SILK SUSPENSION MOVEMENT Pendulum suspended on a silk thread, found in most French 18th- and early 19th-C clocks.

STRINGING Fine strips of contrasting woods inlaid in the wooden case of a clock or piece of furniture.

T

TABERNACLE CLOCK Often tower-shaped clock dating from the 16th C, sometimes with a dial on all four sides.

TOMPION, THOMAS (1638–1713) Probably the most famous English clockmaker, pioneered many new inventions, including the BALANCE SPRING.

TRAIN The series of wheels in a clock or watch MOVEMENT linking the power source (a weight or a spring) to a specific function, such as moving the hands or regulating the strike.

TWO-TRAIN MOVEMENT A MOVEMENT with an extra function, either a striking, musical or alarm train. The first train moves the hands.

V, W

VERNIS MARTIN Form of lacquer patented by Frenchman Guillaume Martin (after whom it was named) and his brothers in the 18th C. It was used for interior decoration and on small objects such as clock cases or boxes.

"WHITE" DIAL Metal clock face that has been painted; found on many clocks after *c.*1775. Also known as a JAPANNED dial.

INDEX